INCREDIBLY DISGUSTING DRUGS

CRACK AND YOUR CIRCULATORY SYSTEM
The Incredibly Disgusting Story

Claudia B. Manley

the rosen publishing group's
rosen central
new york

Published in 2001 by The Rosen Publishing Group, Inc.
29 East 21st Street, New York, NY 10010

First Edition

Library of Congress Cataloging-in-Publication Data

Manley, Claudia B.
Crack and your circulatory system / by Claudia Manley.—1st ed.
p. ; cm. — (Incredibly disgusting drugs)
Includes bibliographical references and index.
ISBN 0-8239-3389-X (library binding)
1. Crack (Drug)—Toxicology—Juvenile literature. 2. Cardiovascular toxicology—Juvenile literature. [1. Crack (Drug) 2. Cocaine. 3. Drug abuse.]
[DNLM: 1. Crack Cocaine—adverse effects—Popular Works. 2. Cardiovascular System—drug effects—Popular Works. 3. Substance-Related Disorders—therapy—Popular Works. WM 280 M279c 2001] I. Title. II. Series.
RA1242.C75 .M36 2001
                                                    00-012140

Manufactured in the United States of America

CONTENTS

Introduction

Kids face a lot of different challenges and stress today. You might be worried about being popular and whether you're hanging out with the "in" crowd. Or you could already be worried about getting into college. Each year, more and more kids are introduced to drugs at a younger age. It can be hard to say no, especially if someone you like or respect offers you drugs. However, it's important to know what you're getting into, because if you don't know the consequences, you may not ever need to worry about being popular or getting into college again. Your worries will be a lot more serious.

We've all learned a lot about the dangers of smoking cigarettes. We know that it causes lung cancer and emphysema, and that it can kill people. Can you imagine choosing to smoke something even more deadly, something that could cause death immediately? Well, that's what crack is.

This book will take you on a trip, an educational one that will help you make the right choices if you are faced with the opportunity to try crack. In 1998, there were about 1.7 million Americans who used cocaine, and almost half a million of those used crack, which is a type of cocaine. While more crack is sold and smoked in cities, it is not just an urban problem. Crack is bought by all kinds of people and sold all over the country.

Many people think that crack is a problem only among poor people, but people of many different incomes, races, backgrounds, and education have become addicted to crack. Sometimes people think they're too smart to become addicted, while others think they're too healthy to die. All these people are wrong. It doesn't matter if you're the richest, most educated,

Olympic superstar; you can still become dependent upon crack cocaine or die from using it.

And it's not popular only with adults. More and more kids are trying crack, and it's not just high school kids either. In 1999, 4.7 percent of all eighth graders said they had tried some type of cocaine, and that was an increase since 1992! These are kids who are twelve to fourteen years old. The group with the highest percentage of users is the age group eighteen to twenty-five, but junior high and high school kids are adding to the numbers. In fact, the average age of kids who have tried cocaine is fourteen.

Although crack cocaine may produce an intense high, one that gives you immediate feelings of alertness and euphoria (feeling really good and happy), the high wears off almost before you can repack your pipe. The physical damage, however, can last a lot longer. Your body can suffer damage that it may never recover from—damage that could kill you.

1 A History Lesson

Crack is a form of cocaine; the effects of crack and powdered cocaine are the same. When autopsies are done on bodies, the coroner cannot tell whether it was crack or powdered cocaine that was used. The way the drug is taken and how quickly it is absorbed into the user's body are the only differences between crack and cocaine.

Powdered cocaine is usually taken by snorting it through the nose, although it can also be shot into the veins (called intravenous drug use) or swallowed. When it's snorted, it is absorbed into the bloodstream through the tissues that line the nose. Injecting it sends it straight into the blood and quickly throughout the body. "Shooting up" is the fastest way to get cocaine into your bloodstream, but smoking crack is the second fastest way. When using crack, the smoke is sent into the lungs where it is immediately picked up by the blood. However, no matter how cocaine is delivered to the blood, it's going to cause a lot of damage.

Smoking crack is the second fastest method of delivering cocaine into the bloodstream.

A LONG TIME AGO. . .

Cocaine—the official name is cocaine hydrochloride—comes from the leaves of a South American shrub called the *Erythroxylon coca.* The leaves of this bush have been chewed, smoked, and mashed into a paste for many centuries and for many different purposes. In the South American Andes—a mountain chain that runs from the bottom of South America up to Venezuela—some people still chew the coca leaves or brew them into a tea. Taken in small amounts like this, cocaine's effects are much like those of caffeine. It keeps people from getting tired,

Cocaine is harvested from the *Erythroxylon coca* plant, which is indigenous to South America.

increases their mental alertness, and raises their energy level. Because it has not appeared to cause major physical or social problems, the governments that are responsible for the Andes region have not limited its use.

In pre-Columbian times (before Christopher Columbus came to the Americas), the Incas used the leaves for medical, religious, and social purposes. It was not used by the common people but reserved for royalty. When the conquistadors came from Spain, they forbid anyone to eat coca leaves. But that was only until the Spanish experienced the effects of coca leaves for themselves.

The Spanish then brought the plant back with them to Europe, where it was believed to help cure all kinds of problems. It was used to fight depression, help cure asthma, and as a treatment for people addicted to opium. In addition, cocaine has an anesthetic quality, which means that it numbs areas that it touches. This reduces feelings of pain. Because of this effect, it was used in products like toothache medicines and tonics.

COMING TO THE UNITED STATES

Cocaine's use spread across Europe during the nineteenth century and eventually came to the United States. It was legal and sold over the counter at pharmacies, just like aspirin is today. It was even an ingredient in Coca-Cola until 1905! Back then, people didn't know about the many problems of cocaine use.

People also smoked cocaine legally. In the early part of the twentieth century, some drug companies sold cigarettes and cigars that contained cocaine. They were generally recommended for therapeutic, or health, reasons. They also didn't contain very much cocaine, maybe .5 or 1 percent. The cocaine that is sold illegally these days is much stronger.

The U.S. government started looking at the results of cocaine use more closely when it was discovered that people could become addicted to it. Its link with the crime world also caused the government to give it a closer look. In 1906, the Pure Food and Drug Act banned the use of cocaine for any nonmedical purposes.

Today, cocaine is a Schedule II drug. This means that only doctors can use it for legitimate medical reasons; for instance, as a local anesthetic—a painkiller that is put on a specific area, like the mouth for tooth surgery.

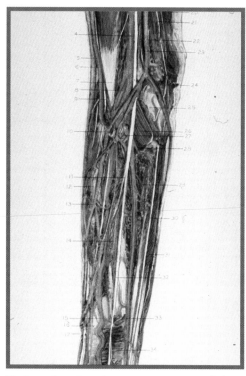

Injection is the most powerful and fastest way to get cocaine into the bloodstream.

ADDICTS FIND NEW WAYS TO GET HIGH

While it may have become illegal, cocaine didn't go away. In addition to the development of a black market to smuggle cocaine from South America into the United States, addicts began to look for other ways to abuse the drug. The most popular way to use it is by sniffing, or snorting, it, but since it is easy to develop a tolerance to the drug, new and faster ways to absorb it were needed. Shooting cocaine directly into the veins was an option, but a lot of people were afraid of using needles. Finally, a stronger, smokable form was developed. This combined the speed of intravenous absorption obtained by shooting up with the ease of snorting it.

Cocaine, in its powdered form, does not simply consist of dried up coca leaves. In order to get it to the white powdered form that is found in the U.S. drug market, the leaves are mashed up with a solvent and partially dried. Hydrochloric acid is then added to this paste mixture, which is then dried completely. The end result is a white powder that is snorted, swallowed, or injected.

Because the effects of the drug are lost by the time it turns into smoke, cocaine in its white powder form is usually not smoked. To make a smokable form, cocaine powder is mixed into a solution that is then boiled. This boiling removes the hydrochloride, the chemical base of cocaine that makes it difficult to ignite. While boiling, a solid substance separates from the rest of the mixture. This is removed and allowed to dry. After it has dried, it's broken into little pieces, and the result is either crack or freebase cocaine.

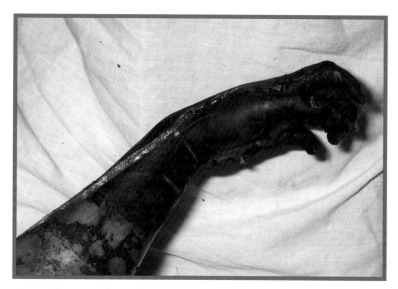

Comedian Richard Pryor suffered third-degree
burns, like the ones pictured here, while freebasing.

At first, the processing of cocaine into a smokable form
produced the original freebase cocaine. Crack is a form of
freebase cocaine. Freebase cocaine was originally made by
adding a solvent, like ether, to burn off the hydrochloride. A
solvent is something that helps dissolve substances. For
example, nail polish remover acts as a solvent. But the use of
solvents added an element of danger that had nothing to do
with the actual effects of cocaine. Sometimes, when smoking cocaine, the solvents that were added would catch fire.
In 1980, comedian and actor Richard Pryor suffered third-
degree burns over half of his body while freebasing.

The first form of crack was reportedly developed in the Dutch Antilles in 1980. Instead of solvents, a base of baking soda, water, and rum was used to burn off the hydrochloride. Today, baking soda and water are the most common ingredients in producing crack. Sometimes ammonia is used, too. Crack got its name because of the cracking sound it makes when burned. Crack is not as highly purified as freebase cocaine, but the vapor that comes from crack when it is smoked is almost pure cocaine.

Crack became a drug of choice in the 1980s, but during the 1970s, cocaine was very popular. Cocaine was considered a hip "status" drug because it was very expensive. The development of crack changed that. The relative cheapness and availability of crack accounts for part of its popularity. The speed with which the body absorbs it is another reason. Plus, the addictiveness of crack keeps people coming back for more. Crack can also make a lot of money for drug dealers. More people can get high from a gram of crack than from the same amount of powdered cocaine, and then they come back for more.

2 A Low for Your Circulatory System

Okay, so you know it gets you high quickly and that people can become dependent on it, but you haven't found out the physical price you pay. Your body can experience many cardiovascular problems, meaning your heart and circulatory system can suffer greatly. However, before we talk about that, let's see how crack works.

HOW DOES IT WORK?

Crack is usually smoked in a pipe, but it can also be added to tobacco or marijuana. The heat of the flame under the pipe bowl (or in the cigarette) causes the cocaine to vaporize, or change into a cloud of smoke. The vapors are inhaled into the lungs and absorbed into the

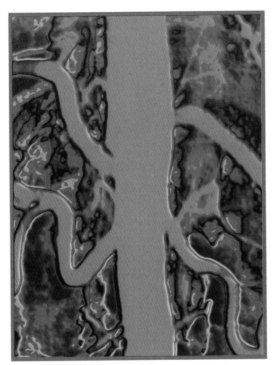
Smoking crack delivers a cocaine high faster than snorting it.

bloodstream. A high from smoking occurs much faster than one from snorting—it's almost as fast as injecting it directly into the veins.

Cocaine is a stimulant, not a narcotic. Narcotics make you feel mellow and depress your system, but stimulants rev everything up. When you smoke crack, it interferes with chemical messengers in your brain. Cocaine intensifies many of your normal body functions, causing your system to perform as if it were in overdrive.

Dopamine is a chemical messenger that's associated with pleasure and movement. It sends signals within your brain that let you know something feels good. Usually, it is released, travels in the brain, and then is reabsorbed. Cocaine, however, blocks this recycling of dopamine and causes it to build up in the brain. This is why cocaine users experience an extreme sense of well-being, also known as euphoria. Smoking crack sends these dopamine blockers into your brain almost immediately.

Cocaine affects the body differently depending on how much you take. The higher the level of cocaine, the more intense its effect on the body. That's why the levels in the leaves and teas eaten and drunk in the South American Andes cause a low level of stimulation to the body, like coffee might. With increasing dosages, the high is not only more intense, but the negative effects are, too. People can go from feeling really good and powerful to becoming nervous, suspicious, or sleepless. But, even worse, the damage to your circulatory system is tremendous.

YOUR CIRCULATORY SYSTEM

Your circulatory system consists of your heart and blood vessels—veins, arteries, and capillaries. It's what gets your blood circulating all around your body so that your organs and tissues get the nutrients and oxygen they need. Basically, the circulatory system is the health highway for your body.

Your circulatory system functions as the delivery method for your body. All the vitamins, minerals, and other

HOW LONG IS THE HIGH?

When you smoke crack, the vapors are absorbed into the pulmonary circulatory system, the system that takes air from your lungs and sends oxygen to your blood cells. These vapors are sent straight to the brain, so the effects are almost instantaneous. It often takes less than ten seconds to feel the high. But the faster the high, the shorter it lasts. Highs from smoking crack last only five to ten minutes while the high you get from snorting lasts fifteen to thirty minutes.

nutrients that you get from food, as well as the oxygen you breathe in, are delivered to all the organs, tissues, and cells by the circulatory system. It is a continuous loop that delivers the good stuff and removes the waste. Without a properly functioning circulatory system, your body can suffer extreme harm—organs can be damaged, tissue can die, and your heart can't function properly.

Your Heart

The heart is the main terminal for your blood. As the engine that keeps the blood flowing, the heart is the most important organ in your circulatory system and your body. If your heart stops, so do you.

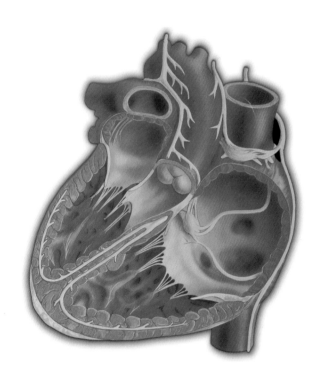

Cocaine use is a severe threat to the proper functioning of the human heart.

The heart has four main sections: the right and left ventricles and the right and left atria. It acts like a pump that pushes the blood through all the veins, arteries, and capillaries in your body. From the heart, blood travels through the pulmonary artery to the lungs. Here it exchanges carbon dioxide (which your body can't use) for oxygen (which fuels your body). The carbon dioxide is released from the body when you exhale and the oxygen that you've inhaled is passed to the blood and carried throughout your body.

Arteries and Veins

Arteries carry blood away from the heart, and veins bring it back. The blood moving away from the heart has all the ingredients your tissues and organs need to thrive. The blood in your veins is "used" blood, moving back toward the heart to get a refill of oxygen and nutrients. But before it gets there, it goes through the liver and kidneys, which filter out all the waste products. The liver and kidneys are very important organs because they help keep your bloodstream clean.

Capillaries

The capillaries are the smallest of the blood vessels. The walls of the capillaries are very thin, which makes it possible for gases (like oxygen and carbon dioxide) to pass through them. This is how oxygen and carbon dioxide, as well as nutrients and waste, are exchanged in the bloodstream.

CRACK IN THE CIRCULATORY SYSTEM

Usually, your body gets oxygen delivered to it via your blood, but when you smoke crack, the cocaine gets delivered around your body as well. So, what does that

Cocaine can lead to a heart attack because it can cause blood vessels and arteries to constrict tightly.

mean? It means that you could have a heart attack, develop a blood clot, or get something called arrhythmia.

Heart Attacks

Studies have shown that cocaine causes cells in the blood vessels to release endothelin, which makes the vessels shrink up, or constrict, quickly and tightly. This slows down, and can even stop, the heart's blood supply. People who smoke crack are at a greater risk for sudden heart attacks because crack causes the coronary arteries—the biggest ones, close to the heart—to constrict. It's like when you bend a garden hose that has water flowing through it. All the water stops because it can't get through the space that has been made smaller, but it keeps pushing anyway. In the same way, blood pressure is increased in your body as the blood tries to pass through constricted arteries. This, combined with a raised heart rate, is a recipe for disaster.

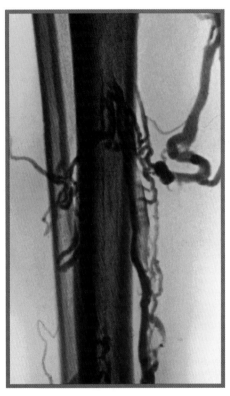

Crack can cause clots to form in the bloodstream.

Blood Clots

Blood clots can form quickly after crack use. Blood clots are masses of blood cells. Crack causes a greater number of red blood cells than usual to start rushing around the bloodstream. This increase in cells causes the blood to be "stickier," which increases blood's tendency to clot. Blood clots behave a bit like snowballs. At first they can move through your bloodstream, and they may sometimes break up along the way. But as cells continue to stick together, the clump just continues to grow until it gets stuck in a vein or artery. This blocks the vein, and then no blood can flow past it. The organs, which depend on fresh oxygen and nutrients, will suffer. This blockage can cause heart attacks and strokes.

Arrhythmia

Arrhythmia, or abnormal heart rhythm, is yet another problem associated with crack use. Arrhythmia happens when the electrical conduction system of the heart, which regulates the beat, is interrupted or disrupted. There are different types of arrhythmia—your heart can start beating too fast, or it can suddenly be too slow, or it might just have an irregular beat. Your heart pumps the regular way it does because this is the best way for your body to get the blood circulating. Changing that can be very dangerous. If your heart doesn't pump enough blood regularly, your body can suffer organ damage.

Your body is an incredible machine, many different parts of which are linked together by the circulatory system. With each inhalation of crack vapors, the drug is delivered throughout your body, changing the way it normally functions. By smoking crack, you mess with the circulatory system's main engine room (the heart) as well as with the delivery of fuel (nutrients and oxygen) by your circulatory system. However, that doesn't cover all the damage. We'll soon discuss the effects of crack on other organs, as well as on your mental state.

3 Your Body and the Effects of Crack

We've just gone over crack's effects on the circulatory system, and you probably think that these are bad enough. Unfortunately, the damage doesn't stop there. Crack can damage your lungs, stomach, and brain, as well as change your moods and your mental health.

LUNGS

Because crack is smoked, it affects your lungs. You may have difficulty breathing or experience respiratory failure. Smoking a combination of crack and tobacco or marijuana makes the damage worse. Imagine coughing up black gunk. Pretty gross, huh? But that often happens to crack users. Smoking crack will give you chest pain and can even cause

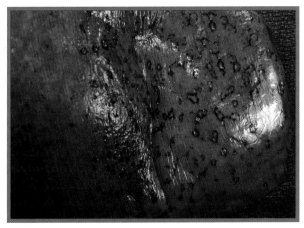

hemorrhaging—bleeding—in the lungs and lead to pneumonia, a serious and sometimes fatal lung condition.

Internal bleeding in the lungs is just one of the dangers crack users may face.

STOMACH AND INTESTINES

Some of the gastrointestinal (dealing with the stomach or intestines) effects of crack include abdominal pain and nausea. You might experience spasms, which are uncontrollable twitches and muscle movement, or feel as though your intestines are burning. Crack can also cause your stomach to bleed. How good can you feel if you're going to throw up? As we'll discuss later, crack also suppresses your appetite.

STROKES

Not only can crack cause major headaches, but users often also have seizures or strokes. A stroke is what happens when you lose brain functions because your brain isn't getting

Diseases such as lung cancer are made worse by crack use.

enough blood. It is also the result of constricting blood vessels and increased blood pressure. Strokes from cocaine (and crack) use are most common in men under forty years of age.

DON'T MIX AND MATCH

Unfortunately, people who abuse crack are often using other drugs at the same time, like tobacco and alcohol. Tobacco, as we already know, does major damage to your lungs and is linked to cancer and emphysema. It also hurts the cells that line your lungs, and the damage is made even worse when combined with crack.

When mixed with alcohol consumption, crack cocaine can become even more deadly. This combination causes the liver to produce something called cocaethylene, which makes the high more intense, but also raises the risk of sudden death. Remember the liver and kidneys?

Well, not only can they suffer damage from crack alone, but alcohol abuse is also one of the leading causes of liver and kidney problems.

Cocaethylene increases the bad effects of cocaine. While the aftereffects of crack can last for about thirty minutes, cocaethylene extends the symptoms of crack use for up to two and a half hours. It can also interfere with the rhythm of your heart, causing arrhythmia. Studies have shown that by combining alcohol consumption and crack use, you multiply your chances of sudden death by eighteen!

PSYCHOLOGICAL AND BEHAVIORAL EFFECTS

You might think that it's bad enough that smoking crack can totally mess up your circulatory and pulmonary (lung-based) systems, but there's more. We haven't talked about the changes in behavior and mood that many people dependent on crack experience.

Depression

Because crack heightens feelings of happiness, people have wrongly thought that it helps depression. But we already know that this high lasts only a very short period of time.

After the high wears off, users often find themselves even more depressed than before. Instead of feeling better, they feel worse and now only want to get more crack. This post-high depression is often referred to as "coke blues."

Paranoia

Crack users also become paranoid and restless. Paranoia is when you think that everyone's against you. If you think that everyone's trying to keep you from scoring more crack, you won't trust anyone and you'll be antagonistic— mean and rude—to those around you.

Users can also be irritable, or easy to anger, and have short tempers. People who are aggressive and sometimes violent when they're not on drugs will often become very violent after smoking crack. Under the influence of the drug, a lot of crack users end up doing things they regret later. Most abusers spend their time trying to figure out how they'll get their next hit.

Crack causes people to become confused and anxious in addition to being depressed. This can lead some users to commit suicide. Some find that they have to smoke crack just to feel "normal"—there's no more high for them, but the depression and anxiety without crack is too much for them to handle. Can you imagine doing something that's so bad for your body just to feel regular again?

Cocaine Psychosis

As is the case with most drug abuse, crack can cause isolation and alienation—feeling removed and distant—from your family, your friends, and all the other aspects of your life. How can there be room for anything else when you're consumed by the need to score more crack? Also, since users require an ever increasing amount to get high, it can get expensive. Many users end up

Chronic crack users may experience formication, which is the feeling that insects are crawling on your skin.

stealing from their friends and family just to buy more crack.

Over time, chronic users can experience cocaine psychosis, a mental condition that changes how you see the real world. This combines paranoia with hallucinations, seeing or hearing things that aren't really there, and a condition called formication. Formication is the sensation that insects are crawling on your skin. Can you imagine how gross that would be? This psychosis can contribute to suicidal behavior.

Other Symptoms

Other symptoms associated with crack use are loss of appetite, loss of performance ability, and a loss of

ATHLETES AND CRACK: NO REPEAT PERFORMANCE

Some people think that because their bodies are in good shape, they can handle the effects of smoking crack. But just because their hearts are in good condition doesn't mean that they won't be affected.

Because crack brings on such an intense high and makes a person feel less tired and more revved up, some athletes have used it to get ready for games. In fact, boxers, basketball players, football players, hockey players, and swimmers have used it. They think that crack can give them a performance edge that their opponents don't have.

In reality, cocaine reduces the amount of time an athlete can perform. Oxygen is really important for the muscles, and crack interferes with the delivery of oxygen. The effects of crack raise the heart rate, too. The heart has to work extra hard because not only is the body doing something really physical, like playing basketball or swimming, but the cocaine has replaced some of the oxygen that the blood cells need. Think about all the other effects of crack that we've already discussed and you'll understand why it wouldn't help an athlete.

Unfortunately, many athletes still believe they can't be hurt by it. Smoking crack has not only hurt star athletes but it has killed as well. Crack doesn't care what shape you're in.

The EKG at the top is that of a normal heart, while the one at the bottom is the erratic heartbeat of a crack user.

Crack users may experience a feeling of power, which can cause them to engage in dangerous behavior.

interest in anything except crack. The loss of appetite accounts for the skinny stereotype of the crackhead and can lead to malnutrition. One experiment involving lab rats showed that they would choose cocaine over food even if they were starving!

Suicide

Many deaths that are cocaine-related result from the psychological changes users experience. The low experienced by many after the use of crack can lead to suicide. This is a particular danger for those using crack as a way to escape depression.

The feeling of power many users experience can lead to high-risk activities like reckless driving or dangerous stunts, such as jumping off bridges or trying daredevil tricks. In addition, the feeling of well-being often leads to unprotected sex, which can cause the spread of sexually transmitted diseases like AIDS.

Crack cocaine can touch many different areas of your life—both physical and psychological. It's hard to imagine that a drug

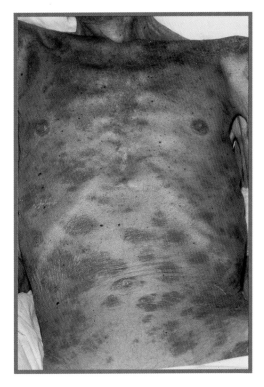

Many crack users feel invincible and engage in high-risk behaviors, ending up with AIDS and other diseases.

that supposedly makes you feel so good can bring you down in so many ways. And if it wasn't bad enough that it can kill you through its effects on your body, it can also lead to suicide because of the way it affects your mind.

In the next chapter, we'll talk about ways that people who abuse crack can overcome their addiction and get their lives back together.

4 Treatment

Unlike heroin, withdrawal from crack doesn't have major physical effects. It's much more psychological; it brings on feelings of depression, anxiety, and isolation. Many crack users believe that they're not addicted because they don't use the drug all the time, but any repeated use can signal a dependency. Crack addicts often go on binges, where they smoke a lot at one time and then stay away from it for a little while because they feel guilty about the binge. But they always return for another binge.

GETTING OVER ADDICTION

Unfortunately, there's no easy way for crack addicts to overcome their addiction. The National Institute on Drug Abuse is looking for a medication that can block or reduce the effects of cocaine. A drug that would help get rid of the severe craving that crack causes is being researched as well.

Some addicts respond well to antidepressants while going through withdrawal. This helps them with one of the worst parts of addiction: the constant attempt to escape depression that's just made worse by using the drug.

Acupuncture, the therapeutic Chinese practice of placing needles on very specific points of the body, has been used to help people stop using drugs. The way the needles are placed helps the chi, or energy, of the body flow. If an addict has been experiencing a lot of problems with his or her stomach, the needles can direct energy there. Acupuncture has been used to reduce the anxiety or fear that many addicts feel when they stop using. It has also been used to help lower their cravings for crack.

THERAPY

Most addicts have to go into some kind of behavioral treatment, a therapy that helps them change the way they feel about and view the drug. Some therapies that

TROUBLE WITH THE LAW

As if all the physical and psychological problems aren't enough, being involved with crack can also land you in jail.

Congress has made tougher sentences for people involved with selling crack because of the violence that is associated with it. Powdered cocaine is usually sold in large quantities in private settings, but crack is sold directly on the street in smaller, individual amounts. The amount of crack on the street and the competition between dealers contribute to even more violence.

There are other ways crack causes violence. We've already discussed how behavior can change and how people who are using crack can be short-tempered and paranoid. Combine this with the need to get another fix and it can lead to trouble. The more crack an addict does, the more he or she wants it. While small amounts of crack might seem inexpensive, it adds up, and often addicts run out of money. To get more money to buy crack, addicts might try to rob people. Because of the state of mind people are in when they are on crack, these robberies can involve weapons and therefore be more violent. When you're addicted to crack, you just don't care what happens to other people.

If you are caught with a lot of crack and the police think you're going to sell it, you will be spending a lot of time in jail. Individuals caught with five grams of crack spend five years in jail.

Possession of crack will land you in prison.

But just because you try crack doesn't mean you're suddenly going to go to jail, right? Well, there is a mandatory prison sentence of one year for just having crack on you. It doesn't matter if you were just holding it for your friend or getting ready to smoke it. You will spend a year in jail!

have worked for crack addicts, particularly young ones, are behavioral therapy, multidimensional family therapy, individualized drug counseling, supportive-expressive psychotherapy, and relapse prevention therapy.

Behavioral Therapy

Behavioral therapy is, in the most basic terms, the removal of bad behavior, like drug use, by showing and rewarding good behavior. Avoiding situations that remind the individual of drug use and not hanging out with the people who he or she used to do drugs with are behaviors that are rewarded on this road to staying off drugs for good.

There are three types of control this therapy hopes to give the individual. The first is called stimulus control. The therapist finds ways to help the user avoid situations that are associated with drug use. The second kind of control is urge control. This goes beyond just the physical urge for it. The user has to identify all the thoughts, feelings, as well as places that led to drug use. By recognizing them, the user can learn to change them. The third element is social control, which brings in family members and friends to help the individual become and remain drug-free. This kind of support is really important because it gives the user other people to rely on and turn to for help.

Group counseling is one of the many options for addicts who want to quit crack or cocaine.

Multidimensional Family Therapy

Multidimensional family therapy places the user inside a whole network of family, friends, and community. Like behavioral therapy, it works to replace the drug abuse behavior with good and positive behavior in each of the areas that involve family, friends, and community.

This therapy includes family as well as individual sessions. In the individual sessions, some of the things that are worked on are decision making, problem solving, and communication.

Individualized Drug Counseling

Individualized drug counseling focuses on getting the individual to stop using drugs. One way it tries to do this is by showing the effect drug use has on the individual's family, community, and friends. Individualized drug counseling also sets up short-term goals to help the user and recommends that he or she participate in a twelve-step program. A twelve-step program is when the individual regularly meets with other people who are trying to get over their addictions. By sharing stories and supporting each other, they help each other get off drugs and back into their lives.

Supportive-Expressive Psychotherapy

Supportive-expressive psychotherapy has two main components. The first is to make a user feel comfortable and supported when the person talks about his or her experiences. The second helps the user look at the things in his or her relationships that might contribute to drug use, and works to change any problem areas. These two together help the individual communicate and take control of situations that might lead to drug abuse.

Relapse Prevention Therapy

Relapse prevention is a long-term therapy designed to keep individuals from using again. It uses the learning process to help see how bad behavior, like drug use, developed. It puts a lot of responsibility into the user's hand by emphasizing self-control, including self-monitoring to recognize drug cravings.

A main element of this therapy is working on problems and situations the user might encounter that encourage drug use and giving him or her the tools for dealing with them.

As you can probably tell, it isn't easy to get and stay clean. There's no magic formula. Recovery requires a lot of work from the individual, and it definitely benefits from the support of family and friends. It may take only one or two hits to become addicted, but it can take years—and for many it's a lifetime battle—to get and stay clean.

KEEP IN MIND

Even though crack isn't in the news as much as it was in the 1980s, it is still very popular and it is still a big problem. The chances that you'll encounter someone offering you crack are not as small as we would like them to be. It's important that you keep in mind the price you'd have to pay if you smoked crack.

By now you should know that smoking crack gives you more lows than one high is worth. In addition to messing with your circulatory system, you can ruin your heart, your lungs, your stomach, and your brain by smoking crack. You can hurt your friendships and your family. You can also end up dead or in jail. Ten minutes of feeling really good can't be worth all that, can it?

Your circulatory system is the deliverer of oxygen and nutrients to all parts of your body. A drug like crack, which is delivered through this system, spreads its damaging effects all over. Knowing all the facts, not only about how your circulatory system works but also the effects of crack cocaine, can help you realize just how foolish one hit off the crack pipe can be.

It's hard not to be influenced by what people around you do. If your friends start doing crack, you might be tempted to try it, too. Just remember all the things that were discussed in this book. It can keep you clean and save your life.

GLOSSARY

anesthetic A substance that causes complete or partial loss of feeling.

anxious Feeling worried or distressed about things that are uncertain.

behavioral Having to do with how one behaves.

black market Illegal business of buying and selling.

chronic Lasting a long time.

coronary Relating to the two arteries closest to the heart.

coroner A doctor who examines dead bodies.

emphysema A lung condition that causes difficulty in breathing and makes one more likely to get infections.

euphoria A feeling of extreme well-being.

formication The sensation that insects are crawling on the body.

intravenous Through the veins.

snorting Taking a drug by inhaling it through the nose.

FOR MORE INFORMATION

In the United States

American Council for
   Drug Education
164 West 74th Street
New York, NY 10023
(800) 488-DRUG (3784)
Web site: http://www.acde.org

Co-Anon Family Groups
P.O. Box 12124
Tucson, AZ 85732-2124
(520) 513-5028
Web site:
   http://www.co-anon.org

Cocaine Anonymous
3740 Overland Avenue, Suite C
Los Angeles, CA 90034
(800) 347-8998
(310) 559-5833

Web site: http://www.ca.org
e-mail: cawso@ca.org

Hazelden Foundation
P.O.Box 11, CO3
Center City, MN 55012-0011
(800) 257-7810
Web site:
   http://www.hazelden.org

Nar-Anon Family Groups
P.O. Box 2562
Palos Verdes Peninsula,
   CA 90274
(310) 547-5800
Web site: http://www.
   onlinerecovery.org/co/nfg

Narcotics Anonymous
P.O. Box 9999
Van Nuys, CA 91409

(818) 773-9999
Web site:
    http://www.wsoinc.com

National Clearinghouse for
    Alcohol and Drug
    Information
P.O. Box 2345
Rockville, MD 20847-2345
(800) 729-6686
Web site:
    http://www.health.org

National Council on
    Alcoholism and Drug
    Dependence
12 West 21st Street, 7th
    Floor
New York, NY 10010
(212) 206-6770
(800) 622-2255
Web site:
    http://www.ncadd.org

National Families in Action
Century Plaza II

2957 Clairmont Road,
    Suite 150
Atlanta, GA 30329
(404) 248-9676
Web site:
    http://www.cc.emory.edu/
    NFIA

In Canada

Canadian Centre on
    Substance Abuse
75 Albert Street, Suite 300
Ottawa, ON K1P 5E7
(613) 235-4048
Web site: http://www.ccsa.ca

Canadian International Drug
    Awareness Centre
1093 Millwood Court
Orleans, ON K1C 3E9
(613) 830-7366
Web site:
    http://www.freenet.
    carleton.ca/cidac
e-mail: cidac@ncf.ca

FOR FURTHER READING

Bayer, Linda N. *Crack and Cocaine*. Philadelphia: Chelsea House Publishers, 2000.

Berger, Gilda, and Nancy Levitin. *Crack*. New York: Franklin Watts, 1994.

Carroll, Marilyn. *Cocaine and Crack*. Springfield, NJ: Enslow Publishers, 1994.

Chier, Ruth. *Danger: Crack*. New York: PowerKids Press, 1996.

Holmes, Ann. *Psychological Effects of Cocaine and Crack Addiction*. Philadelphia: Chelsea House Publishers, 1999.

Peck, Rodney G. *Crack*. New York: The Rosen Publishing Group, Inc., 1991.

Robbins, Paul R. *Crack and Cocaine Drug Dangers*. Springfield, NJ : Enslow Publishers, 1999.

Shulman, Jeffrey. *Focus on Cocaine and Crack: A Drug-Alert Book*. Frederick, MD: Twenty-First Century Books, 1990.

Turck, Mary. *Crack and Cocaine*. New York: Crestwood House, 1990.

INDEX

CREDITS

About the Author
Claudia B. Manley is a freelance writer living in Brooklyn, NY, with her partner, son, and cat.

Photo Credits

Cover and page 16 © Alfred Pasieka/Science Photo Library, cover insert © Custom Medical Stock Photo; pp. 8, 9 © Wesley Bocxe/Photo Researchers, Inc; pp. 11, 13, 21, 25, 26, 31 © 2000 Custom Medical Stock Photo; p. 16 © Alfred Pasieka/Science Photo Library; p. 19 © David Gifford/Science Photo Library; p. 22 © Salisbury District Hospital/Science Photo Library; p. 29 © Francois Gohier/Photo Researchers, Inc; p. 32 © Mahaux Photo/Image Bank; p. 33 © Dept. of Medical Photography, St. Stephan's Hospital, London/Science Photo Library; p. 37 © VCG 1993/FPG; p. 39 © B. Daemmrich/The Image Works.

Series Design
Laura Murawski

Layout
Danielle Goldblatt